The Making of a Champion

A World-Class
Ice Skater

David Curtis Preston

www.heinemann.co.uk/library
Visit our website to find out more information about **Heinemann Library** books.

To order:
☎ Phone 44 (0) 1865 888066
▤ Send a fax to 44 (0) 1865 314091
▣ Visit the Heinemann Bookshop at www.heinemann.co.uk/library to browse our catalogue and order online.

First published in Great Britain by Heinemann Library, Halley Court, Jordan Hill, Oxford OX2 8EJ, part of Harcourt Education. Heinemann is a registered trademark of Harcourt Education Ltd.

Editorial: Geoff Barker, Rebecca Hunter and Dan Nunn
Design: Ian Winton
Illustrations: Peter Bull
Picture Research: Rachel Tisdale
Consultant: Andrew Elliot
Production: Duncan Gilbert

Originated by Ambassador Litho Ltd
Printed in China by WKT Company Limited

ISBN 0 431 18936 6
08 07 06 05 04
10 9 8 7 6 5 4 3 2 1

British Library Cataloguing in Publication Data
Preston, David Curtis
A world-class ice skater – (The making of a champion)
1.Skating – Juvenile literature
2. Skating – Training – Juvenile literature
I. Title
796.9'1
A full catalogue record for this book is available from the British Library.

Acknowledgements
The publishers would like to thank the following for permission to reproduce photographs:

Corbis pp. **10** (Jeff Kowalsky), **17 top** (Don Mason), **19 top** (Chris Trotman), **19 bottom** (Craig Ambrosio), **20** (Bettman), **29 top** (Cory Sorensen), **30** (Neal Preston), **31 bottom** (Eddy Lemaistre), **32** (Robert Laberge), **33 top** (Peter Jones), **33 bottom** (Brian Leng), **39** (Chris Trotman), **40** (Paul Sutton); Empics pp. **4**, **5 right**, **12** (Tony Marshall), **13, 22, 24**; Getty Images pp. **5 left** (Mike Powell), **6** (Express Newspapers), **7** (Allsport), **9** (Chris Niedenthal), **11** (Frederick M. Brown), **15** (Pierre Andrieu), **16** (Matthew Stockman), **17 bottom** (Doug Pensinger), **18** (Brian Bahr), **21** (Bob Martin), **23 top** (Yuri Kadobnov), **23 bottom, 25** (Doug Pensinger), **26** (Clive Brunskill), **27** (Trevor Jones), **28** (Steve Kagan), **29 bottom** (Tony Duffy), **31 top** & **34** & **35 both** (Yuri Kadobnov), **36** (Ronald C. Madra), **37** (Bob Martin), **38 top** (Steve Powell), **38 bottom** (Doug Pensinger), **41** (Pascal Rondeau), **42** (Bill Greenblatt), **43 bottom** (Robert Laberge); Mary Evans Picture Library p. **8**.

Cover photograph reproduced with permission of Duomo/Corbis.

The publishers would like to thank Liz Littler of NISA U.K. for her help in the production of this book.

Every effort has been made to contact copyright holders of any material reproduced in this book. Any omissions will be rectified in subsequent printings if notice is given to the publishers.

The paper used to print this book comes from sustainable resources.

Contents

Words printed in bold letters, **like these**, are explained in the Glossary.

The greatest show on ice

Ice skating is undoubtedly one of the world's most spectacular sports. Once a fashionable pastime in Victorian Britain, ice skating – or figure skating, as it is officially known – now attracts some of television sport's biggest audiences. Combining artistry and skill, grace and power it is one of the true tests of an athlete.

Technique and presentation

There is much more to reaching the top in ice skating than merely being able to skate well. Champion skaters are not just judged on whether they can perform a certain manoeuvre – they are also rated on how they perform it. Every year skaters must use a different set of 'moves' or **required elements**, in their set routines. These then have to be set to music. And for those taking part in **pairs** and **ice dance** competitions, a skater will also be judged on how they interact with their partner.

The USA's Sarah Hughes celebrates her surprising gold medal win at the 2002 Olympic Games in Salt Lake City.

The rewards

Ice skating should be fun and is a sport that can be enjoyed by all ages. But to an up-and-coming champion, dedication and mental toughness need to be added to the sheer thrill of skating around an ice rink. The great German champion Katarina Witt first fell in love with skating at the age of five and soon showed a natural talent on the ice. But, to achieve her goal of becoming a world and Olympic champion, she was required to dedicate practically all of her spare time to skating. Witt went on to realize her ambitions and has become one of the sport's first superstars. Behind the glamour and acclaim, however, few will know just how much hard work she had to put in to get to the top.

But the rewards can make all the work worthwhile. As champion skater Michelle Kwan once said, 'Just being out there, being in the moment – that's what athletes dream about. I felt that sweet spot.' The burning ambition for fellow US skater, Sarah Hughes was to be the very best. As a little girl, Hughes once said: 'My dream is to be in the Olympics and get a gold medal. I can't wait for that to happen.' As she stood on the gold medal podium at the 2002 Olympics in Salt Lake City, her dream turned into reality.

With five world titles to her name, Michelle Kwan is one of the most successful performers in American skating history.

The flair, artistry and athleticism of champion US skater Scott Hamilton have helped turn him into one of the sport's biggest box-office draws.

The start of skating

The birth of the sport of ice skating dates back to the late 19th century. Skating had been a strictly pleasurable pastime but at the start of the 1880s, a number of clubs in Europe began to organize tests and competitions. In 1892, the International Skating Union (ISU) was created to standardize the rules for all figure skating and speed skating competitions. Four years later, the first World Championships for men was held in Vienna, Austria.

Early days

Those early days of ice skating were quite different from the thrilling sport we know today. Although a skater performed a routine containing a few simple jumps and spins, the majority of his marks were received for the 'compulsory figures' – a series of complex tests invented by an Englishman, H.H. Vandervell. In 1902, a women's event was introduced at the World Championships, while the **pairs** competition was introduced four years later. Even so, the feats of early skating stars are still celebrated today. Two basic jumps of modern-day routines, moves called the 'axel' and 'salchow', both date back to the early 1900s and are named after their creators, Axel Paulsen and Ulrich Salchow.

It was not until the second half of the 20th century that skaters began to introduce the athletic leaps and jumps that are now so familiar. In 1951, the American Dick Button performed the first ever double axel in competition, and then amazed the skating world by successfully completing a triple loop the following year.

TV stars

The growing influence of television in the 1960s and 1970s gave skating a far greater prominence in world sport and also helped produce a new breed of skating stars such as Peggy Fleming and Dorothy Hamill from the USA, and the UK's John Curry.

The Olympic and triple world champion Peggy Fleming became one of the USA's most popular sports stars during the 1960s.

New heights

Evidence that the heat of competition can push skaters to even greater heights came during the men's short programme at the 2001 World Championships in Nagano, Japan. Following five near-flawless routines from his main competitors, Russian skater Alexei Yagudin (centre) produced the skate of his life. He landed all his jumps and spins to earn six perfect 6.0 marks. The total was the highest number an individual skater had ever received for a short programme at a World Championship.

This was quite an achievement for someone who confessed to feeling 'sleepy' when he took to the ice!

Television's demands also helped to reduce the emphasis of the 'viewer unfriendly' compulsory figures, which made up 60 percent of a skater's score. Instead greater emphasis was placed on artistry and technical ability.

During the 1980s, skating provided Olympic sport with some of its most dramatic moments. The breathtaking performance of the UK's Jayne Torvill and Christopher Dean in the **ice dance** at the 1988 Winter Games earned them skating's first ever perfect score of nine straight 6.0 marks. Katarina Witt also proved that technical excellence and glamour could be combined to awesome effect on an ice rink.

As ice skating moved into the 21st century, so too have its stars continued to take the sport to new heights. Triple jumps for women and quadruple jumps for men are now the norm for individual routines. The likes of Michelle Kwan and Sasha Cohen from the USA, and Evgeni Plushenko and Alexei Yagudin from Russia, are setting the standards for a whole new generation of ice kings and queens.

Equipment

The first ice skates, using animal bones strapped to leather footwear, are thought to have been developed over 1500 years ago as a form of travel in the frozen lands of northern Europe. Nowadays ice skates come in many shapes and sizes but the basic principles of design have remained the same down the centuries.

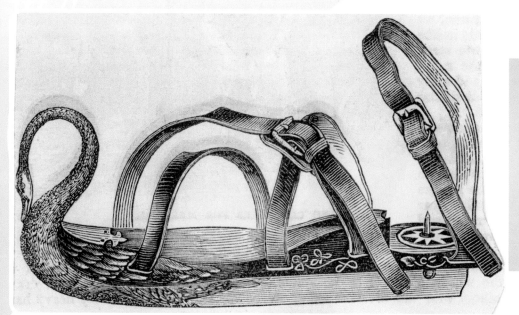

Until the invention of metal blades in the 19th century, skaters wore wooden platform skates attached to boots by leather straps. This example, the Royal Albert, dates back to 1851.

Selecting a boot

Ice skates can be expensive, so it is always advisable to be sure that skating is for you before investing in a pair. The majority of ice rinks offer skates for hire, though the quality may vary because of intensive use, so always ask for a selection and look for any signs of wear and tear. The other vital piece of equipment is socks. Straightforward sports socks are by far the best bet here – skaters should never be tempted to use thick, woolly ones. Some skaters choose to wear a boot bare-footed, although this can be harmful to the foot if it is not a perfect fit.

When the time comes to buy a new boot, a skater needs to be sure it is one that they are comfortable with. Despite the potential expense involved, it is always better to select the right size – buying a larger boot and growing into it may help cut costs but it will also make skating that much harder before the boot fits properly. A well-fitting boot should allow the skater to wiggle their toes without the whole foot moving. All new skates should have their blades sharpened before use.

The cheaper alternative, particularly for younger skaters whose feet are still growing, is to buy used skates. Naturally, the quality can vary so skaters should watch out for worn blades as well as rips and tears in the leather.

Each of the three major ice sports – figure skating, speed skating and ice hockey – require specialized skates, each with their own unique features.

Edges fact

Skaters often talk about 'inside' and 'outside' edges of a blade. These are simply the parts of the blade that face in or out, depending on the direction of travel. However, different moves, jumps and turns are performed with them, so learning the correct terms is important from the beginning.

Figure skate

Toe pick

The figure skate gives maximum ankle support while the blade has a toe pick to help skaters make jumps.

From the most inexperienced skater to a world champion like German skater Katarina Witt (below), the right footwear will improve performance and help avoid injury.

Hockey skate

The shorter blade on ice hockey skates enables players to stop far more quickly than figure skaters.

Speed skate

The long blade on the speed skate offers maximum speed but the boot provides little protection for the skater.

First steps

Regardless of whether someone is a world champion or just an occasional weekend skater, ice skating is first and foremost about having fun. There is nothing quite like the thrill of moving on ice and just about every champion there has ever been, first took up skating for the pure enjoyment of it.

Getting experience

Before setting foot on ice for the first time it is advisable for new skaters to get some experience of wearing and walking in skates. Skaters can purchase 'guards' for the blades, which enable first-timers to get used to the feel of them. A few simple knee-bends and balancing alternately on one leg will also make the experience of moving on ice less scary. A low centre of gravity is crucial to maintaining control on ice.

A young skater taking to the ice for the first time should never try to be over-ambitious. Just about all newcomers will head to the barrier and hold on to it tightly! This is fine as it enables them to practise knee-bends and get used to the new sensations beneath their feet. However, once the confidence builds, new skaters should try to leave the 'comfort zone' of the barrier and stand on their own two feet. Once again, they may repeat their knee-bends and experiment with lifting one skate off the ice.

The secret for any young skater on their first few visits to the rink is to concentrate on feeling relaxed on ice rather than trying any complex moves. As the 1997 World Champion, Tara Lipinski recalls: 'I was a little wobbly the first time I put on figure skates and stepped on to the ice as a six-year-old, but by the time I got off, I knew figure skating was it for me. I was hooked.'

A young Tara Lipinski develops her balance and flexibility with ballet teacher Marina Sheffer. Despite a rather wobbly introduction to ice, Lipinski went on to claim the ladies' world title in 1997.

Most skaters will take to the ice for the first time at a public rink. Holding on to a friend may well be the best option for the first few steps but do be prepared to take the odd tumble.

Learning to fall

To the novice skater, falling over is always one of the greatest fears. But even the most skilled performer will take the occasional tumble when skating. The following points should be remembered:

1. If a skater senses he is losing his balance, he should try to touch his toes – this helps to regain the correct centre of gravity.

   If he is unable to regain balance, he should tuck his chin into his chest. This will minimize the chances of him banging his head on the ice.

2. The skater should bend his knees and keep as low as possible, before sliding on to his bottom – this will help to make the impact with the ice far softer.

3. To regain his footing, the skater should start by getting on all fours. He should then bring one skate on to the ice followed by the other, using the hands as support.

1.

2.

3.

Dedication

Reaching the very top in ice skating, like so many other sports, requires a huge amount of time, dedication and effort and – more often than not – plenty of money. Lessons, coaching, practice sessions, competitions and travel can place great burdens on a skater (and their family) both physically and financially – but they are all essential in the development of a potential champion.

Learning the lessons

Lessons are essential for any would-be skater, regardless of their goals or ambitions. The majority of ice rinks throughout the world offer basic tuition from experienced skaters. This is the ideal way to grasp the basics as well as to determine individual abilities and aspirations.

If a young skater is serious then he or she will need to be prepared to dedicate a great deal of spare time to the sport. More advanced lessons – and even the hiring of a personal coach – will be required along with practice, and then more practice. Most national associations run a series of tests to monitor a skater's progress. In the USA, for example, skaters are not allowed to take part in competitions without having passed the relevant test. These are graded on a rising scale from pre-preliminary to senior level.

Town support

During his early years of skating, Todd Eldredge had to rely on the generosity of the residents of his home town in Chatham, Massachusetts. By organizing a series of fundraising events, they were able to help Todd develop into a world champion. The grateful Eldredge has since repaid the favour by donating money to the town of Chatham to help other young athletes realize their sporting potential.

Family sacrifices

Michelle Kwan first fell in love with ice skating at the age of five after watching her elder brother Ron playing ice hockey. Along with her older sister Karen, Michelle (seen here with her father), became a dedicated and enthusiastic skater. However, the burden placed upon Michelle's parents was a heavy one. Faced with having to fund the ambitions of three children, they were forced to sell their restaurant business and their home to meet the massive expenses. Without such dramatic sacrifices from her parents, it is doubtful whether the four time ladies' world champion would have made it to the top of the sport.

Helping hands

Up until the fall of the Soviet Union in the early 1990s, skaters from the Communist bloc countries in eastern Europe enjoyed one massive advantage over their western counterparts. Potential champions were selected and groomed from an early age – their government funded all aspects of their skating development and training. In Europe and North America, however, the majority of young skaters were, and still are, forced to rely on the generosity of families, friends and local businesses.

As ice skating remains essentially an amateur sport, taking part in competitions can be a costly and time-consuming experience. A skater will usually have to compete in a host of local, regional and national competitions based on his or her 'skill' levels before even thinking about national and international events. And even when skaters do make it to the very top, they cannot afford to relax – a fact summed up by Russia's Alexei Yagudin, who once said: 'I know if I want to win, I have to work hard.'

Moving on ice

When watching a champion skater on television, one may get the impression that moving about on ice is easy. But this is because the skater has put a lot of time and effort into mastering the basics of skating. Balance and control are very important for any would-be champion and these are essential before a skater can think about attempting any jumps or spins.

Balance

The secret to any form of skating, from starting as a beginner to becoming a champion, is balance. Good body posture is essential. Because ice is obviously slippery – and an ice skate is designed to take advantage of this – the slightest change in weight can cause instability or a fall. Without a good posture, skaters cannot make quick directional changes or even attempt to spin or jump.

Posture

The correct skating posture involves keeping the knees bent, the chin up and the stomach tucked in. This helps to keep the body weight centred over the front half of the skate blade (see 1 below). The hands should also be held out, about 90° from the body at about waist height (see 2). Once a skater feels confident with this, they should then try standing on alternate feet (see 3). The relationship between the shoulders and the hips is also vital – they should always remain parallel with each other and should never be rotated separately even when standing on only one blade.

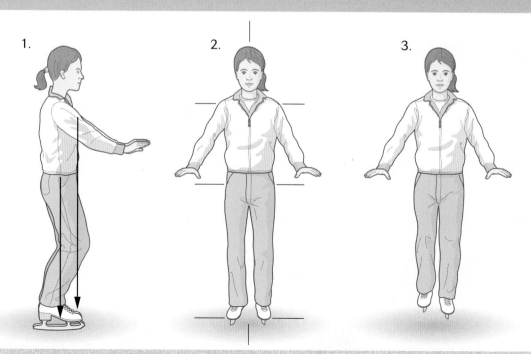

The duck walk

The duck walk is the simplest way of moving around on ice. This is achieved by keeping the heels close together and the toes pointing out – rather like a duck. The best way to start is by stepping a few centimetres forward, gradually gathering momentum as the confidence grows.

Pushing and gliding

Effectively, there is only one way to push off in figure skating: the inside edge push. This is done by placing the weight over the skating foot and keeping the front part of the 'inside' edge of the blade in contact with the ice (see below).

As this is done, the other foot is lifted off the ice and is brought forward and placed on the ice. This motion is known as gliding (see below). Skaters also glide with both feet on the ice to slow them down if they have pushed off too fast.

glide

Stopping

There are several ways to stop on ice but the easiest to perfect is known as the 'snowplough'. This is the same method used by skiers and involves bending the knees and keeping the feet parallel before pushing the front of the feet inwards into a slight pigeon-toed position.

push

The secret behind moving well on the ice is to maintain good balance, as demonstrated here by US skater Sasha Cohen.

Coaching and development

When a skater graduates from group lessons, he or she is then faced with a decision that could well shape the rest of their skating career. A good instructor or coach will effectively control the majority of their skating time, so selecting the right one is a choice that needs plenty of consideration. There are thousands of coaches worldwide, many of them former champions themselves and all are looking out for a future star.

Establishing targets

Before approaching a coach, a skater needs to be clear about just how far they want to go and how much time they want to commit to the sport. The rising young American skater Parker Pennington began skating at the age of three and had private lessons at the age of eight. However, as his skills advanced, Pennington began to realize the need for a coach. During a summer visit to relatives in Ohio, Pennington persuaded his parents to take him to visit the former world and Olympic champion, and leading coach, Carol Heiss-Jenkins. As he recalls: 'I had seen her on television and liked her style and personality. I asked my parents if I could take lessons from her.' Heiss-Jenkins also liked her pupil and helped Pennington to become the first man to claim US titles at juvenile, intermediate, novice and junior levels.

The coach's role

A coach will help establish a lesson and practice schedule appropriate to the skater's goals and abilities. A general rule of thumb is that for each 15 minutes of lesson time, a skater should have at least 30 minutes of practice time to reinforce those

US talent Parker Pennington is one of many young skaters who have been guided by respected coach Carol Heiss-Jenkins.

Selecting a coach

A good way to select a coach is to visit other rinks to watch coaches training and see how they work. Skaters can also get in touch with their national association who will give them a list of qualified teachers in their area. They should remember to:

• check that their coach has the necessary qualifications

• check out the coach's methods with other students

• be sure that they have good communication skills

• talk over any goals with their prospective coach and ensure that they can offer the right amount of commitment.

A skater will spend a great deal of time with a coach so they must be happy that the two of them can work together – but they should also be prepared to do what they are told!

lessons. Lessons are usually given in 15, 20 or 30 minute portions, depending on the skater's needs, the demands upon the coach's commitments and the length of time skaters are allowed on the ice. In addition, a coach will also advise skaters on their off-ice training schedule.

Decisions about testing and entering competitions are usually left to the coach, who will plan out all areas of the skater's programme, from selecting and preparing music to ensuring that the routine meets the technical requirements of the event. A good coach will help guide the skater through the warm-up, as well as providing any last-minute advice or support – this is known as 'putting you on the ice'.

Leading coach Robin Wagner (left) helped guide her young charge Sarah Hughes (right) to Olympic gold in 2002.

The key jumps and spins

Ice skating involves an enormous variety of moves and techniques that are progressively learnt throughout a career. At the very top, the most spectacular moves are the jumps and spins which all elite skaters use in their repertoires – either on their own or as **combinations**. Some of these jumps are discussed over the next two pages.

The jumps

There are two types of jump: a 'toe jump' where the skater uses the toe pick at the front of the skate to push off into the air, and an 'edge jump' where the skater takes off from a particular edge of a skate without the benefit of help from the other skate. A single, double, triple or quadruple jump refers to how many times the skater spins in the air between the takeoff and landing.

Toe loop

In the toe loop, the skater glides backward on the outside edge of the right skate, jabs the left toe pick into the ice, and then rotates to the left.

Flip

The flip is a similar jump to the toe loop, but the skater glides backwards on the inside edge of the left skate and toepicks with the right foot to start the leftward rotation.

Lutz

The most difficult toe pick jump is the lutz. It is very similar to the flip

2004 Canadian champion, Emanuel Sandhu, is pictured in mid-air during a dramatic moment in one of his routines.

jump except that during takeoff the skater tilts or leans the gliding boot onto an outside edge rather than an inside edge. This outward lean is what makes the lutz more difficult than the flip.

Loop

The loop is easy to identify because the skater crosses one leg before the other before rotating – rather than using his toe pick to launch himself as with the toe loop.

Axel

To do the axel jump the skater takes off from the left front outside edge. This is the only jump with a forward takeoff but it ends with the skater going backwards on a right outside edge. It is really a $1\frac{1}{2}$ rotation jump.

Salchow

The salchow jump takes off from the left back inside edge then scoops the right leg up and over the left to initiate the jump rotation. Being able to swing the right leg around to gather momentum helps to make this the easiest of the edge jumps.

Cross-toe spin

The most popular type of spin – often used to bring a routine to an end – is the cross-toe. In this move, the skater stands upright with the legs crossed. The arms are held overhead or in front of the body while the skater turns.

Camel or parallel spin

Another common type of spin is the camel, in which the skater spins on a straight leg while the other leg and torso are parallel to the ice. There are several variations on this spin: the 'flying camel' where the skater jumps

Leading US skater Sasha Cohen performs a layback spin, a required element in the ladies' short programme.

before settling into the spin; the 'Hamill camel' which involves moving directly from a camel into a sit spin; and a 'catch-foot camel' where a female skater arches her back to grab the blade of her free leg.

Sit spin

In a sit spin, the skater bends one leg, lowering into a sitting position, while extending the other out in front while spinning.

Layback spin

The layback spin is a **required element** for women. The body either leans backward or sideways while the free leg is bent and lifted diagonally toward the back.

The 1994 Olympic ladies' champion, Oksana Baiul from the Ukraine, is pictured here performing a camel spin.

The compulsory figures

Although no longer part of major competition, the compulsory or 'school' figures remain the technical core of ice skating. Requiring the skater to trace a series of figure '8's on the ice, the compulsories are essential in helping a skater to control both edges of a figure skate.

Major influence

The very first school figures were set down by H.H. Vandervell in the early 1880s. Although the figures were the supreme test of technical ability, the tests were of limited appeal to spectators who preferred the thrills and spills of the long programmes. In 1973 their influence towards a competitor's overall score was downgraded and by the start of the 1990 season, they were removed altogether from senior competitions. Even so, elements of the compulsories continue to be used by national skating associations for testing and ranking the skills of skaters.

All figures are performed by pushing off from a stationary start. Once they are moving, a skater is required to **trace** a figure eight on one skate – there are an amazing 70 different variations – without stopping or touching the ice with his or her free leg until the tracing is completed. There are also stipulations as to which 'edge' of the skate a skater can use – touching the surface with both edges, or 'flatting', is not allowed. Judges then examine the tracings made by the skater, and deduct marks if they do not meet an exact, perfect pattern.

Although there are 70 variations of the figures, these can be whittled down to six main forms.

Austria's Trixi Schuba is widely recognized as the best there has ever been in the compulsory figures.

1. The three

The three requires the skater to make a turn at the top of each circle of the '8'. This is achieved by changing edges on the skate while also changing direction.

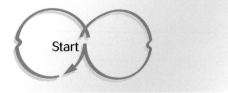

Start

2. The double three

In this figure, a skater must perform two turns on each circle, once again with a change of direction and edge.

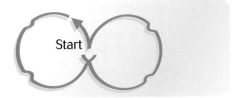

3. The loop

Using the same edge, and without changing direction, the skater traces a small loop within each circle.

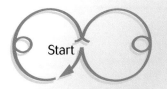

4. The bracket

The bracket is similar to the three except that the skater is required to change edges at the top of the circle but without changing direction.

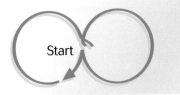

5. The rocker

In the rocker, an extra loop is added to the '8'. Each of the three circles is traced in a different direction without changing edges.

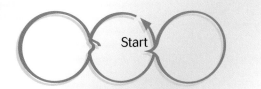

6. The counter

Once again, the counter requires an extra circle. This is performed by changing direction with a half-turn.

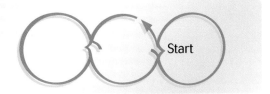

All the exercises (except no. 3) are skated on circles that are about three times the height of the skater. The loop is done on circles that are about the same height as the skater.

The disappearance of the compulsories in competition skating has shifted the emphasis towards more flamboyant performers but the figures will always be the supreme test of technique.

Although she won world gold in 1989, Japanese skater Midiri Ito found the compulsory figures very difficult during her early years on ice.

Singles skating

The oldest and, to many, the most dramatic form of skating competition is the singles. Pitting skater against skater, it is the ultimate test of skill, artistry, technique and – in more recent times – innovation.

On your own

Unlike in **pairs** and **ice dance** competitions, the solo skater stands and falls by his or her own skills and mistakes – and it can be a nerve-wracking and solitary experience. As the former world champion Brian Orser has commented: 'I'm not convinced there is any consecutive four and a half minutes in sport as lonely as a competitive figure skating programme.' But, just as equally, the end of a well-executed performance can provoke very different emotions, especially for another Canadian skater, Elvis Stojko, who claims that: 'Pain is short-lived, but pride lasts a lifetime.'

Since compulsory figures were scrapped, all singles skating competitions require two separate displays from a skater – a short and a long programme.

One of the most flamboyant male skaters of recent times is Elvis Stojko, 'The King of the Quads'.

The short programme

The short programme is worth one-third of the overall score and requires a skater to perform a number of stipulated moves within their routine. Skaters are allowed to select their own music (within certain guidelines) but the routine has to be performed within two minutes and 40 seconds. At the highest level, both men and women have to execute two jumps, a jump combination, three spins and two step sequences. In competitions higher marks can be achieved for successfully completing more complex moves but any failure will result in the automatic deduction of marks. Each judge awards two separate marks. These are for **required elements** reflecting difficulty and how well a skater performs a move; and **presentation**, which reflects the judge's opinion of the skater's style, interpretation of the music and overall harmonious composition of the programme.

The long programme

Also known as the free skate, the long programme enables skaters to demonstrate their full range of skills and moves. Nowadays, the world's leading stars will perform at least six triple jumps, a number of spins and some triple-triple combinations – while many of the men have also started to introduce quadruple jumps into their routines. Skaters are judged on technical expertise, style, quality of movements, proper use of the available space and overall composition. Only two triple or quadruple jumps may be repeated and these are only given marks if they are part of a **combination** or sequence. Once again, two sets of marks are awarded: one for **technical merit**, and one for presentation.

Julia Sebastyen, a Hungarian skater, on her way to winning the ladies' gold at the 2004 European Championships.

Quadruple jump star

Canadian skater Kurt Browning may have captured four world titles between 1989 and 1992 but he will be best remembered for his long programme at the 1988 World Championships in Budapest, Hungary. A powerful jumper, Browning had twice attempted – and failed – to perform a quadruple jump earlier in the season. At the Worlds, however, he managed to get everything right, executing a quadruple toe-loop to rapturous applause. In doing so, he had become the first skater in history to perform any kind of quadruple jump successfully in competition.

Pairs skating

No skating event has undergone as many style changes as the **pairs** competition. Originally similar to what we now know as the **ice dance**, the pairs event has developed into a thrilling mix of athletic jumps and graceful balletic moves.

Gradual development

Early pairs competitions were very formal affairs. The skaters, wearing evening dress, performed in tandem and included very few separate moves in their programme. The 1920s saw the introduction of a series of new, daring lifts and individual jumps, which was further advanced by the athletic North American style that developed during the 1950s and was best exemplified by the Canadian pair of Barbara Wagner and Robert Paul.

The ideal pair

In the days of the former Soviet Union, most pairs were put 'together' by the state coaches. This was the case in 1981 when a tiny, shy 11-year-old skater named Ekaterina Gordeeva was paired with Sergei Grinkov, four years her senior. The two youngsters appeared to have little in common with each other, yet they gradually began to develop an instinctive relationship on the ice. That situation suited their coach Victor Ryzhkin who said that 'it is not good for a romantic relationship between pairs. They start to argue all the time.' The pair went on to win four world titles as well as twice claiming Olympic gold – and they also fell in love. They were married and turned professional in 1991 but there was to be no happy ending. In 1995, 28-year-old Sergei collapsed and died of a heart attack whilst practising.

A far more laid-back approach to the pairs emerged during the 1960s through the ballet-inspired performances of the Soviet husband-and-wife team Ludmila and Oleg Protopopo. Irina Rodnina, who claimed a record 10 world titles with partners Aleksei Ulanov and Aleksandr Zaitsev, signalled a return to more athletic performance. However, during the late 1980s, the Russian pair of Ekaterina Gordeeva and Sergei Grinkov fused the two styles together, combining a mixture of daring lifts with grace and elegance.

Skaters who have developed late or have had their careers disrupted by injury (and are thereby unable to reach the top in singles competition), often take up pairs skating as an alternative route to the top. As with singles skating, pairs competitions are divided into a short and a long programme.

Short programme

This programme should contain various set or specified lifts and pair spins, with solo jumps, spins, **step sequences** and a **death spiral** and throw jump. There are two marks from each judge, one for **required elements**, and one for **presentation**.

Long programme

The requirements for the pairs long programme are based on the same principles as for individual skaters. Since skaters compete as a pair the moves must be synchronized and must include lifts, throw jumps, pair spin **combinations** and a death spiral as well as solo elements.

The ice dance

Despite being the first recognized form of ice skating, the **ice dance** is the most recent addition to the international skating roster. It differs from the **pairs** event in a number of ways. Ice dancers are not allowed to incorporate elements that demonstrate feats of strength, open movements that separate the partners, or excessive movements that only link the partners by their hands. Since 1936, the ice dance has been divided into three phases – compulsory dances, original dance and free dance.

Compulsory dances

Each couple performs one compulsory dance. This is selected from a variety of standard ballroom steps such as a waltz or tango. The music is kept to a regular, precise number of beats per minute, and the skaters are expected to skate to the music in strict time. Judging is based on 'accuracy of steps, placement of the pattern, the style and carriage of the skaters and unison'. They are also judged on their timing with the music and their expression of the character of the dance. There are two marks awarded from each judge. One for technique and one for timing and expression. Each dance accounts for 20 percent of a couple's score.

Original dance

The original dance is also a ballroom type dance, but the coach makes up the dance pattern. Each year at the beginning of the season, governing associations select a style of music – such as waltz, swing, tango, and so on – to be used by all teams competing. Generally the style chosen differs from level to level. It is up to the dance couple to choose music that conforms to the rules specified for that season, and to

The Canadian team of Shae-Lynn Bourne and Victor Kraatz added daring athleticism to their routine to win the 2002 Olympic gold.

Golden perfection

One of the most famous performances in ice skating history came during the ice dance at the 1984 Winter Olympics in Sarajevo. When reigning world champion British skaters, Jayne Torvill and Christopher Dean, took to the ice for the free dance, they had already created history by becoming the first pair to receive three perfect 6.0s for a compulsory dance. Dancing to Maurice Ravel's driving classical piece 'Bolero', they produced a stunning performance of intense and sensual brilliance. The judges awarded them three 6.0s in the technical scores and an incredible clean sweep of perfect marks for artistry – a first in Olympic ice skating history.

make up the dance for competition. There are two marks from each judge, one for **composition/required elements** and one for **presentation**. This dance accounts for 30 percent of a couple's overall score.

Free dance

In the free dance the couple must interpret both the rhythm and melody of music selected by them, whilst not using prescribed dance steps. Couples may perform lifts, jumps and spins, but their use is limited. Separations for a maximum of five seconds are allowed, but couples must avoid **mirror skating** and skating more than two arms-lengths apart. At least one skate of each partner should be in contact with the ice at all times except during jumps or lifts. The skaters are marked on their timing, speed, unison and their use of the ice, difficulty, variety and sureness – along with style and interpretation of the music. There are two marks from each judge, one for **technical merit**/required elements and one for presentation. The free dance counts towards 50 percent of a couple's score.

Off-ice training

Although every champion skater will have put in countless hours of work on the ice, the hard graft does not end once they leave the rink – a top performer needs many attributes quite apart from being a skilful skater. Endurance, flexibility and strength are some of the areas on which top skaters will spend their time away from the ice.

Strength training

Strength throughout the body can help in all aspects of skating. It is particularly important for jumps, where controlling the upper body's momentum is important for height. Strong arms also enable a skater to pull in faster during spins to achieve more rotation.

Weight-training is an excellent way to help develop basic strength and muscular endurance. Free weights or machines are available at most gyms but all weights need to be used correctly, so an instructor should always be consulted first. A good weight-training programme may consist of three to four sets of ten repetitions performed over a period of an hour and undertaken two or three times a week. Even the smallest of skaters, such as Michelle Kwan and Kristi Yamaguchi, regularly use weights in their training programme. Sit-ups are also useful for building up the muscles around the centre of the body.

Aerobics

Aerobic endurance training gives skaters the ability to exercise for longer periods – necessary for maintaining performance levels throughout a routine. This training can be done in many ways, such as cycling, road-running, swimming or step aerobics, and is very good for the heart as it burns off excess fat. Ideally, this type of conditioning should be done for four, half-hour periods at least three times a week.

The 1995 US ladies' champion, Nicole Bobek puts a high value on her gym training.

Plyometrics for explosive strength

Various aspects of skating, such as jumps, call upon the body to produce fast, explosive movements. The muscles have special fibres, which help to aid explosive actions, but these fibres need to be stimulated and built up. This is best done through what is known as plyometrics – training which involves a combination of fast movements like skipping, jumping and kicking, and shuttle runs (sprinting in one direction then stopping and sprinting in the other direction).

Sprinting and longer distance running are an integral part of a skater's training routine.

Ballet technique

Ever since the days of the great Norwegian champion Sonja Henie in the 1920s, many top skaters have used ballet techniques as part of their training. As well as

helping a skater achieve grace, artistry and fluid movement, ballet can also help skaters gain greater power for jump height and improve lower-back strength for control. The routines of the great 1976 Olympic champion, John Curry (left), are a particular example of how ballet styles can be used on ice. Other types of dance may also be beneficial, depending on the type of music chosen. Many ice dancers practise ballroom dancing classes to learn how to do the 'real' dance before transferring those ideas back on to the ice.

Stretching and warming up

Although different skaters have many different exercise and training routines, one of the things they will spend a lot of time doing is stretching. Ice skating makes great demands upon the body in terms of muscle use, flexibility and posture – and stretching is essential to all of these.

Getting in shape

Skaters, like almost all athletes, should always stretch before and after taking to the ice. This helps to improve the level of performance and relaxes any tired or tight muscles – lessening the chance of injury. Stretching should also play a regular part in a skater's schedule away from the ice rink.

Flexibility is one of the keys to skating success and regular stretching exercises will help increase a skater's 'range of motion' – the ability to stretch the body as far as possible. This can be particularly useful for performing complex moves such as spirals and layback spins.

There are two basic types of stretch – the 'static' where a stretch is made and then held, and the 'flexible' where the body moves with the stretch, such as with high kicks. General stretches, such as for the legs and arms, are fairly straightforward, but more difficult exercises should never be attempted without consultation with a coach or physiotherapist. The same also applies for a skater who has injured himself. Skaters should always maintain a good posture whilst stretching, and should always try to keep their breathing constant. Furthermore, they should always pull out of a stretch if there is any hint of pain.

The former World and Olympic champion Brian Boitano shows that warming up before taking to the ice is just as important for a champion as it is for a beginner.

Warming up and cooling down

A decent warm-up should consist of 20 minutes of light exercises that will help increase blood flow, pulse and muscle flexibility.

Before undertaking any stretches or strenuous exercise, the body temperature and flow of blood to the muscles needs to be increased. Most skaters do this by gently gliding or **stroking** across the rink for up to 10 minutes. An alternative for beginners, or if rink time is limited, is to do some jogging or light skipping.

Once warmed up, a skater moves on to their routine of stretches. They

Three-time US champion Michael Weiss is famed for his flexibility built up by an intensive training programme.

hold each stretch for ten seconds or so and repeat this five times. A top skater will aim to stretch each of these major muscle groups: quadriceps, hamstrings, calves, shoulders and torso.

After completing their main exercise on the rink, a skater should cool down by continuing to skate while gradually reducing the intensity. This helps to slow the body down to its normal levels. Many skaters will do some gentle stretches within an hour of cooling down – this helps reduce any tension or soreness developing in the muscles.

Sasha Cohen places great emphasis on warming up properly which means she is flexible enough to be able to achieve amazing positions such as this one.

Fuelling up

As ice skating is a power and endurance sport, a balanced nutritional diet plays a vital role in keeping a skater in tip-top condition. Food, and the nutrients it contains, is the 'fuel' that keeps the body running, but every skater needs to be aware of the right kinds of fuel to take on board.

A healthy diet

A strict diet routine is not necessarily required but a good knowledge of healthy eating most certainly is. Some skaters, such as the USA's Jennifer Kirk, rely on their own instincts. 'I wouldn't say that I have any kind of a 'set' diet,' says Kirk. 'I try to eat foods that are good for me. I like a lot of protein. I usually have an egg for breakfast, and I also try to eat a lot of vegetables.' Similarly, Alexei Yagudin does not worry about the quantities he eats. 'I just try to eat healthy foods and avoid the things that seem to take away my energy,' says the Russian champion.

The USA's Jennifer Kirk, one of many skaters who simply choose to eat sensibly rather than follow a rigid diet.

Proteins

Proteins play a key part in helping to build up muscles and general body strength. They help supply muscles with glycogen, which skaters require for sudden bursts of energy. Typical sources for protein include fish, skimmed milk and lean meats such as chicken. The standard recommended daily dose of protein is about 0.5g per half kilo of bodyweight. More may be required if a skater is trying to make more substantial gains in strength.

Carbohydrates

Carbohydrates are the major source of energy for our bodies – but the exact amounts needed can vary depending on activity levels and how quickly a skater's body absorbs them. Whole-grain bread, potatoes and pasta are all good sources and they help stabilize energy levels. The downside to carbohydrate intake is that they will turn to fat if the body does not burn them off through exercise. As a general rule, around 60 percent of the daily calorie intake should come from carbohydrates.

Elvis Stojko's famed flexibility helps him to pull off an amazing array of jumps and spins. Here he performs the Russian splits.

Fibres

The human body needs to be flushed through on a regular basis to rid itself of **toxins**. Intake of fibres, through foods such as whole-grain bread, cereals and oats, will ensure a healthy digestive system. A good guide is to consume between 20g and 30g of fibre a day.

A selection of the foods a skater needs to keep the body fully toned for ice skating competition. One of the most important diet tips is to avoid fried or fatty foods.

Health fact

Essential in helping the body function correctly, vitamins and minerals can be found in many foods, especially vegetables and fruit. A useful guideline is the 'five alive' theory – eating five different portions of fruit or vegetables each day. Calcium, found in milk, is particularly important for skaters because it strengthens the bones.

Skaters also need to keep well hydrated, especially after gruelling training sessions or routines. Water is by far the best source and is far healthier than coffee, tea or high-sugar drinks.

The required elements

Every ice skating competition will require skaters to perform a certain amount of 'moves' within their routine. At the very highest level, these requirements are laid down by the sport's ruling body, the International Skating Union (ISU).

Minor changes and revisions are introduced each season but this is a good guideline as to what a skater needs to be skilled at to compete at championship level.

Short programme – singles skating

In the short programme all skaters are required to perform eight moves or elements. The requirements vary slightly between the men's and women's competitions, but in general consist of three jumps (such as the double axel, or a triple jump); three spins (for example, a flying spin, or a spin **combination**); and two **step sequences**.

Short programme – pair skating

The **required elements** for the **pairs** short programme are based on the same principles as for the singles. They include an overhead lift, a double twist lift and side-by-side double or triple jumps carried out in unison. There is one spin combination and a throw jump. A **death spiral** is required on a specific edge that changes each season. The final element is a step or spiral step sequence.

Long programme – singles skating

The long programme requires the same moves for both men and women. Skaters may make any number of jumps. They must also do at least one but not more than three jump combinations or sequences of jumps. A minimum of four spins is

Russia's Elena Liashenko pulls off a jump combination as part of her long programme.

The Polish pair of Dorota Zagorska and Mariusz Siudek demonstrate an overhead lift.

Ice dance

In the **ice dance** competition the specified steps are the required elements for the compulsory dance section. In original dance, the required elements are: a minimum of two dance lifts, one dance spin and two different step sequences. In the free dance, a couple must include between one and three dance spins within the routine. They are also required to perform between two and seven lifts, including one rotational lift and one non-rotational lift with a change of edge. In addition, they must carry out two series of twizzles (synchronized foot movements) and two different step sequences. The ISU announces exact requirements each year.

required including one spin combination and one flying spin. One step sequence must cover the full ice surface. Finally they must do one sequence of 'moves in the field' which generally includes spirals and spread eagles.

Long programme – pairs skating

The pairs long programme must include between three and five lifts, a **throw** jump and a pair combination spin as well as a solo jump, a jump sequence, a solo spin, a step sequence and a moves in the field. All elements should be skated by each partner in unison.

Tanith Belbin and Benjamin Agosto of the USA perform one of the lifts required in the ice dance.

Preparing for competition

Every ice skating season usually requires a new series of routines to be planned and perfected by the skater. For singles and **pairs** skaters this means that two brand new routines have to be created, while the compulsory dances have to be performed to stipulated pieces of music.

Planning

The starting point for skaters and coaches alike is to ensure that their new routines contain all the elements required by the sport's governing bodies. This all has to be set to music and choreographed into a smooth, seamless performance. The free skate and free dance allow far greater scope for experimentation but even these have to be performed within certain guidelines.

Nowadays, most top skaters will also call upon the services of **choreographers**. Their skills can be wide and varied – some are former skaters while others may come from a ballet or dance background.

Music

Musical selection is vital to bring out the very best of a skater's talents. One of the most popular sources of music down the years has been the opera 'Carmen'. The striding rhythms of Bizet's classic have been interpreted for countless free skating routines – most famously during the 1988 season when different parts from the piece were used by the world's two leading female skaters, Katarina Witt and Debi Thomas. The choice for the **ice dance** competition is rather more limited. The compulsory dance has to be performed to an agreed piece of music while the set routine requires a certain style of music to be selected.

Debi Thomas of the USA, whose technical skills and flair for musical interpretation helped her to claim the 1986 world title.

Battle of the Brians

During the 1980s, Brian Boitano was rightly regarded as one of the world's most technically gifted performers. But while the US skater could pull off a string of complicated moves, his routines seemed to lack the artistic flair and appeal of his

great rival Brian Orser. For the 1988 Olympic season Boitano and his long-term coach Linda Leaver called upon the additional services of former pairs skater Sandra Bezic. Together they came up with a new short programme which saw Boitano portray the character of a cocky youth showing off his skills. His long programme, performed as a young army officer (left) achieved all the moves – including his trademark **tano lutz** – but also displayed a real sense of artistry. The new routines worked wonders and helped Boitano to pip Orser to gold at both the Olympics and World Championships in what the press dubbed the 'Battle of the Brians'.

Another area to consider in selecting music is how much the judges will like the piece. Although medleys from rock and pop songs have become more popular in recent years, there is still a feeling that a more traditional selection will earn better marks. Four-time world champion Alexei Yagudin certainly believes that many judges have a subconscious preference for classical music. 'I think if someone skates to classical music, he will be one step higher than the guy who skates to modern music.'

Judging and scoring

Just about the most controversial – and complicated – area of competition ice skating is the scoring and judging system. Even skaters sometimes struggle to understand its finer points. A new system has now been introduced to make things a little clearer and, hopefully, a lot fairer.

The traditional system

The traditional '6.0s' system of scoring has been used in ice skating since the 1920s. Although it has often been modified and updated down the years, the basic principles remain the same. Nine judges give two sets of marks for each skater in each phase of the competition. The quality and difficulty of a skater's performance is assessed. The maximum score is 6.0. In each

The scoreboard shows the nine perfect '6.0s' awarded to Britain's ice dance duo Torvill and Dean at the 1984 Olympics.

phase, the two marks are added together and these totals are then used to determine a skater's 'ranking'. For example, a skater that receives 5.6 for the **required elements** and 5.7 for **presentation** in the short programme would get a total of 11.3 points from that judge. However, a skater's ranking is not determined by his total points but by where he is ranked by each judge in relation to the other competitors.

The judges watch the men's competition at the 2002 Olympics in Salt Lake City. They are selected by the ISU from nine different countries.

New Judging System

The New Judging System, which was developed by the ISU following the judging controversies at the 2002 Olympic Games (see panel below), was introduced as a trial system for a selection of events in the 2003 season. In the new system twelve judges will be used. Each skater starts with zero points and is then awarded marks for each element of their programme according to an agreed scale. Points are added or subtracted (based on an assessment by the judges of the quality of execution of each element), according to strict guidelines. At the end of the programme, the judges also award five marks for presentational aspects of the performance, such as **choreography** and transitions from one move into another. Scores for each of a skater's programmes are added together and the highest score wins.

Golden controversy

Undoubtedly the most controversial judging incident in skating history came at the 2002 Olympic Games in Salt Lake City. The battle for the gold medal in the **pairs** competition was between the 1999 world champions, Elena Berezhnaya and Anton Sikharulidze from Russia and the Canadian pair Jamie Sale and David Pelletier (below) – the reigning world champions. The Russians were first to skate in the long programme but their routine was hampered by two flawed moves. Even so, the judges still marked them highly, awarding a mixture of 5.8s and 5.9s. Sale and Pelletier were the final pair on the ice and proceeded to put in a near perfect performance of pairs skating which left the 30,000 spectators chanting 'six point oh, six point oh'. However, the judges seemed to be the only people in the arena who disagreed and once again awarded 5.8s and 5.9s. When the scores were compared, the Russians had amazingly been placed first by five of the nine judges and thereby took the gold medal.

Amid claims that the French judge had been put under 'undue pressure' by Russian officials, the Canadian team appealed against the result, and Sale and Pelletier were eventually awarded a gold medal as well. The furore led to the overhaul of the judging system which brought about the introduction of the New Judging System.

The major championships

For the world's elite skaters, much of the international skating season is all about the 'big ones' – the World Championships and, every four years, the Olympic Games. These are the only two events where all of the world's top performers come together to compete head-to-head.

The skating season

The ice skating season starts in September and runs through until the spring, culminating in the 'Worlds'. There are other international competitions including a series of Grand Prix events, though many skaters will only compete in one or two, as they continue to practise and perfect their routines. Europe's best will always aim to compete at the European Championships, while for other nationalities, the Four Continents is the major championship outside the 'Worlds'. Many national championships serve as the qualifiers for the World Championships, with the top two or three performers earning selection for their team.

The World Championships

The World Championships place immense demands on a skater. With a qualifying skate followed by two competition days (three for the **ice dance**), skaters have little time to relax. They have to concentrate on perfecting their programmes but also

Gold medal winner Alexei Yagudin (centre) stands proudly alongside runner-up Evgeni Plushenko (left) and Tim Goebel, during the 2002 Olympic Winter Games.

have to keep an eye on the performances of the other competitors. Many championship routines have been changed at the last minute in an attempt to make them more attractive to the judges than their rivals. And it's under this great pressure, with millions watching on television, that the true champions come into their own, producing skating of breathtaking quality.

The Olympics

For many skaters, being chosen to skate at the Winter Olympics is almost more important than competing at the World Championships. The will to win is just as strong but even for the skating greats, making it to the Games is an achievement itself. Looking back on her gold medal-winning performance at Nagano, Japan in 1998, Tara Lipinski recalls: 'I wanted to squeeze every experience I could out of the Games. I wanted to live the Olympics.' Olympic competition can also squeeze that little bit more out of a skater. Robin Cousins (UK) and Annett Poetzsch (Germany) in 1980, and Sarah Hughes (USA) in 2002 have all claimed Olympic golds without managing to win a world title.

Skating scandal

The tensions and intense rivalry that can sometimes be present in ice skating were revealed to the whole world in a famous incident at the US National Championships in 1994. With the Olympic Games just around the corner, two of the world's leading female skaters, Tonya Harding and Nancy Kerrigan, were preparing to go head-to-head for the ladies' title when Kerrigan was assaulted after a practice session.

Kerrigan was struck on her knee by an assailant, and the resulting injury forced her to pull out of the competition – which Harding went on to win. Police investigations later revealed that Kerrigan's attack had been planned by Harding's ex-husband and her bodyguard – who claimed that the skater had approved the plot. Despite speculation that Harding might be left off the Olympic team, both

skaters lined up to do battle at the 1994 Winter Olympics in Lillehammer, Norway.

With the eyes of the world upon them, the two women enjoyed very different fortunes. Harding (right) struggled throughout her programmes and eventually finished eighth. Kerrigan (left), however, was at her best and only lost the gold medal to Ukrainian Oksana Baiul by a highly controversial judging decision.

Six months later Harding was stripped of her national title and banned from the sport for life by the US Figure Skating Association.

On top of the world

Reaching the top of their chosen profession is the peak of achievement for any athlete. For ice skaters it is a just reward for many years of dedication and, invariably, financial outlay. Winning a World Championship or Olympic title carries no major financial reward but it does earn a skater the acclaim and respect of peers and fans.

Professional skating

Ever since the 1920s, there have been a host of professional ice skating shows that offer a variety of on-ice entertainments. In the days where the 'amateur status' of skaters was strictly controlled, appearing in such shows was the only way a top performer could earn any kind of living from the sport. Touring shows like Champions on Ice, Stars on Ice and Holiday on Ice have proved immensely popular with audiences and they allow skaters to pull off moves, such as backward flips, which are not allowed in International Skating Union (ISU) competitions.

In the USA, in particular, spectacular shows have become a regular part of the TV schedules, introducing new generations to the skating skills of some of the greatest champions of ice skating.

Stars on ice

One of today's leading shows is the spectacular Stars on Ice tour. Founded by Scott Hamilton in 1986, Stars on Ice has always attracted the world's leading skaters and nowadays features both former and current champions performing side by side. Here, Hamilton performs a routine with former Olympic champion Kristi Yamaguchi.

For many years, the distinction between an amateur, or 'eligible', and professional, or 'ineligible', ice skater was very clear: anyone who took money for teaching or performing would automatically lose their amateur status. However, during the 1990s the ISU began to relax regulations for skaters 'eligible' to compete in their competitions. In addition, they also introduced prize money for certain events such as the Grand Prix competitions.

Appearing in an unsanctioned professional competition is effectively the only activity that the ISU now defines as being off-limits for eligible skaters. As long as they have the permission of their national federations, eligible skaters can now be paid for appearing in ice shows and competitions, making endorsements and TV appearances, and also coaching.

Champions and records

The three premier competitions in international ice skating are the World Championships and the European Championships which are both held annually, and the Olympic Games which take place every four years. The Europeans are limited to skaters from Europe but have nevertheless featured world-class performances from some of the sport's biggest stars, particularly during the days of the Soviet Union. The World Championships and Olympics, however, bring together skaters from all over the globe, enabling the top performers from North America and Asia to join the battle for skating supremacy.

2004 World Championships – Dortmund, Germany

Men's	
Medal	Skater/Country
Gold	Evgeni Plushenko RUS
Silver	Brian Joubert FRA
Bronze	Stefan Lindemann GER

Ladies	
Medal	Skater/Country
Gold	Shizuka Arakawa JPN
Silver	Sasha Cohen USA
Bronze	Michelle Kwan USA

Pairs	
Medal	Skater/Country
Gold	Tatiana Totmianina & Maxim Marinin RUS
Silver	Xue Shen & Hongbo Zhao PRC
Bronze	Qing Pang & Jian Tong PRC

Ice Dance	
Medal	Skater/Country
Gold	Tatiana Navka & Roman Kostomarov RUS
Silver	Albena Denkova / Maxim Staviski BUL
Bronze	Kati Winkler & Rene Lohse GER

2004 European Championships – Budapest, Hungary

Men's	
Medal	Skater/Country
Gold	Brian Joubert FRA
Silver	Evgeni Plushenko RUS
Bronze	Ilia Klimkin RUS

Ladies	
Medal	Skater/Country
Gold	Julia Sebestyen HUN
Silver	Elena Liashenko UKR
Bronze	Elena Sokolova RUS

Pairs	
Medal	Skater/Country
Gold	Tatiana Totmianina & Maxim Marinin RUS
Silver	Maria Petrova & Alexei Tikhonov RUS
Bronze	Dorota Zagorska & Mariusz Siudek POL

Ice Dance	
Medal	Skater/Country
Gold	Tatiana Navka & Roman Kostomarov RUS
Silver	Albena Denkova & Maxim Staviski BUL
Bronze	Elena Grushina & Rustan Goncharov UKR

2002 Olympic Games – Salt Lake City, USA

Men's	
Medal	Skater/Country
Gold	Alexei Yagudin RUS
Silver	Evgeni Plushenko RUS
Bronze	Timothy Goebel USA

Ladies	
Medal	Skater/Country
Gold	Sarah Hughes USA
Silver	Irina Slutskaya RUS
Bronze	Michelle Kwan USA

Pairs	
Medal	Skater/Country
Gold	Elena Berezhnaya & Anton Sikharulidze RUS
	Jamie Sale & David Pelletier CAN
	(Tie for gold medal)
Silver	Not awarded
Bronze	Xue Shen & Hongbo Zhao PRC

Ice Dance	
Medal	Skater/Country
Gold	Marina Anissina & Gwendal Peizerat FRA
Silver	Irina Lobacheva & Ilia Averbukh RUS
Bronze	Barbara Fusar Poli & Maurizio Margaglio ITALY

Records

Most Olympic Gold Medals		
Catergory	No. Medals	Skater/Country/Years
Men	3	Gillis Grafstrom SWE 1920, 1924, 1928
Ladies	3	Sonja Henie NOR 1928, 1932, 1936
Pairs	3	Irina Rodnina USSR 1972, 1976, 1980 *with two different partners

Most World Championship Medals		
Catergory	No. Medals	Skater/Country/Medals Awarded
Men	13	Ulrich Salchow SWE (10 Gold, 3 Silver)
Ladies	11	Sonja Henie NOR (10 Gold, 1 Silver)
Pairs	10	Irina Rodnina USSR (6 Gold with Aleksandr Zaitsev, 4 Gold with Aleksei Ulanov)
Ice Dance	8	Natalia Bestemianova & Andrei Bukin USSR (4 Gold, 3 Silver, 1, Bronze)
	8	Marina Klimova & Sergei Ponomarenko USSR (3 Gold, 5 Silver)
	8	Irina Moiseeva & Andrei Minekov USSR (2 Gold, 3 Silver, 3, Bronze)

Individual/Free Dance Records	
Record	Record Holder/s
Youngest World Champion	Tara Lipinski (USA) aged 14, 1997
Youngest male Olympic gold medallist	Dick Button (USA) aged 18, 1948
Youngest female Olympic gold medallist	Sonja Henie (NOR) aged 15, 1928
Youngest skater to compete at an Olympic Games	Sonja Henie (NOR) aged 11, 1924
Longest jump	Robin Cousins (GBR) 5.82 metres during Axel jump
Highest scores	Jayne Torvill & Christopher Dean (GBR) 29 perfect 6.0's at 1984 World Championships
Only skater to win two medals in the same Olympics	Madge Syers (GBR) 1908 – Gold in Ladies, Bronze in Pairs

Country abbreviations

BUL = Bulgaria
CAN = Canada
FRA = France
GBR = Great Britain
GER = Germany
HUN = Hungary
JPN = Japan
NOR = Norway

POL = Poland
PRC = People's Republic of China
RUS = Russia
SWE = Sweden
UKR = Ukraine
USSR = Union of Soviet Socialist Republics
USA = United States of America

Glossary

aerobic
involving or improving oxygen consumption by the body

choreographer
a person who creates and arranges programmes for skaters

combination
two skills, such as a jump or spin, performed in an immediate and consecutive order. For example a skater performing a combination jump must not change feet or turn between the two jumps.

composition
marks awarded in the original dance section of the ice dance competition. These reflect how the elements of the dance are put together.

death spiral
a difficult move in which the male holds his partner's hand and pulls her in a circle around him; the female glides on one foot, with her body nearly lying on the ice

ice dance
an event performed by two skaters performing dances and moves mostly based on ballroom dancing

mirror skating
when two skaters move in such a way that their motions are mirror images of each other

pairs skating
an event in ice skating in which two skaters perform together in unison to accompanying music

presentation
the second set of marks awarded in all events except for the compulsory dances.

required element
the jumps, spins and moves that must be included in a short programme for singles and pairs skaters

step sequence
a series of steps across the ice in straight, circular or 'S'-shaped movements to demonstrate a skater's precision and agility

stroking
a method of gaining speed on ice where skaters push forward from one inside edge to the other inside edge

tano lutz
a variation of a lutz which involves raising one arm above the head whilst revolving in the air. Named after World and Olympic champion Brian Boitano.

technical merit
this mark is awarded in the singles and pairs free skate, and in the free dance. Difficulty, variety, sureness and speed are all factors that are marked.

throw
a move in which the male lifts his partner and throws her away from him. She continues the move with a mid-air rotation, landing on one foot.

toxins
substances in the body that are considered to be poisonous or harmful to the system

trace
make a line on the ice using the skate's blade

Resources

Further reading

Superstars on Ice: Figure Skating Champions, Patty Cranston (Kids Can Press, 1997)

Contains photographs and information on today's leading skaters, as well as a rundown on the history of skating.

Ice Skating Basics, Aaron Foeste (Sterling Publishing, 1998)

Highly illustrated guide to mastering the basics of ice skating, from the first steps on ice to some fancy stops.

The Encyclopedia of Figure Skating, John Malone (Facts on File, 1998)

A comprehensive A-Z of skating champions, technical terms, historical events and competition results.

Useful websites and addresses

www.sk8stuff.com
A detailed guide to all the tests and competitions in the USA.

www.frogsonice.com
A unique guide to all the skating positions as demonstrated by frogs!

www.goldenskate.com
One of the largest resources for figure skating on the Internet.

ice-dance.com
A guide to all aspects of ice dancing.

International Skating Union
Chemin de Primerose 2, CH-1007 Lausanne, Switzerland
Telephone: (+41) 21 612 66 66
Fax: (+41) 21 612 66 77
www.isu.org

Ice Skating Australia Incorporated
P.O. Box 567, Archerfield Qld 4108
Telephone: (+61) 7 32 77 13 31
Fax: (+61) 7 32 77 58 89
www.isa.org.au

National Ice Skating Association of the UK Ltd
National Ice Centre, Lower Parliament Street, Nottingham
NG1 1LA
Telephone: (+44) 115 9888 060
Fax: (+44) 115 9888 061
www.iceskating.org.uk

The United States Figure Skating Association
20 First Street, Colorado Springs, CO 80906-3697
Telephone: (+1) 719 635 52 00
www.usfsa.org

Skate Canada
865 Shefford Road, Gloucester, Ontario K1J 1H9
Telephone: (+1) 613 748 56 35
www.skatecanada.ca

New Zealand Ice Skating Association
P.O. Box 15 838, New Lynn Auckland
Telephone: (+64) 09 625 6424
www.nzisa.com

Disclaimer

All the Internet addresses (URLs) given in this book were valid at the time of going to press. However, due to the dynamic nature of the Internet, some addresses may have changed, or sites may have changed or ceased to exist since publication. While the author and Publishers regret any inconvenience this may cause readers, no responsibility for any such changes can be accepted by either the author or the Publishers.

Index

Titles in the *Making of a Champion* series include:

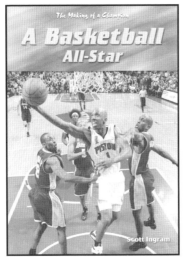

Hardback   0 431 18938 2

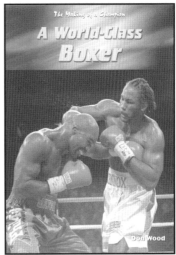

Hardback   0 431 18937 4

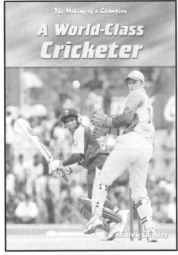

Hardback   0 431 18940 4

Hardback   0 431 18936 6

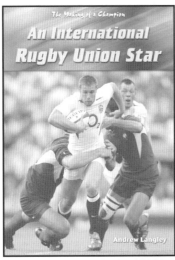

Hardback   0 431 18939 0

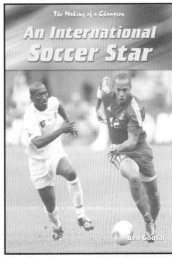

Hardback   0 431 18935 8

Find out about the other titles in this series on our website www.heinemann.co.uk/library